Earth: Slow Changes

Table of Contents

by Melissa McDaniel

Pictures To Think About	i
Words To Think About	iii
Introduction	2
Chapter 1 Glaciers	4
Chapter 2 Water	10
Chapter 3 Wind	18
Chapter 4 Wind and Water Work Together	24
Conclusion	30
Glossary	31
Index	32

Pictures To Think About

Earth: Slow Changes

Words To Think About

Characteristics: landform, deep, ?

canyon

What do you think the word **canyon** means?

Examples: Grand Canyon, Bryce Canyon, ?

erosion

What do you think the word **erosion** means?

Latin: **ex-** (away)

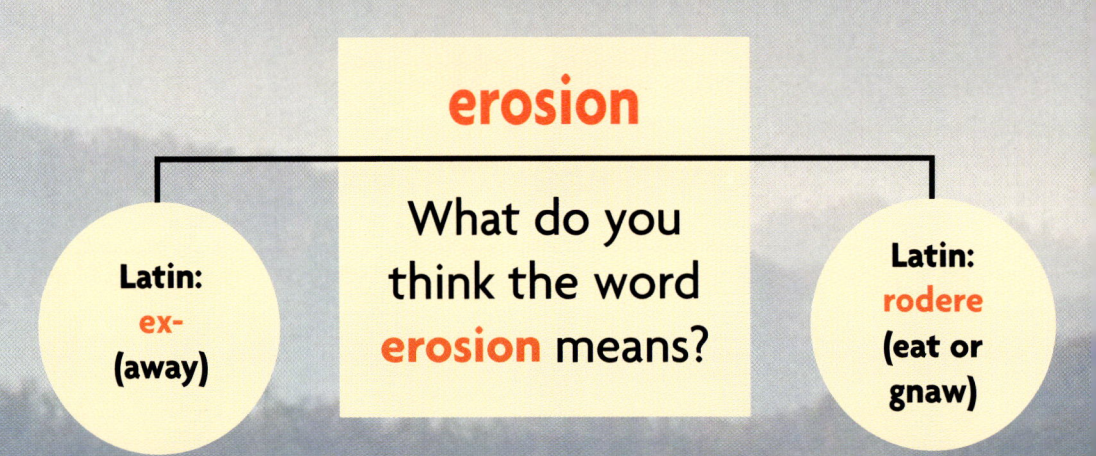

Latin: **rodere** (eat or gnaw)

Read for More Clues

canyon, page 6
erosion, page 2
glacier, page 4

glacier

What do you think the word **glacier** means?

What is a **glacier** made of?
- ice
- ?
- snow

What does a **glacier** do?
- moves very slowly
- ?
- wears away land

iv

Introduction

Pick up a rock. Does it feel hard? A rock can crush things. What about rain? Does it seem powerful? No? Over time, rain can wear away rock.

Think about it. Rain hits the ground. Raindrops break tiny bits of dirt and rock loose. The drops carry the tiny bits with them. The bits slowly wear away Earth's surface.

Wind and ice wear away Earth, too. This wearing away is called **erosion** (ih-ROH-zhun). Read on to find out how erosion has slowly changed Earth.

It's a Fact

The Appalachian Mountains once rose higher than 30,000 feet. Over millions of years, erosion wore them away. Now the highest point in the Appalachians is just 6,684 feet.

▲ The Appalachian Mountains seem tall today, but they were much taller before erosion wore them down.

CHAPTER 1

Glaciers

▲ Glaciers cover almost all of the huge island of Greenland.

Think about a piece of ice as big as a mountain. What would happen if that mountain of ice started to move? It would flatten everything in its path.

Giant chunks of ice that move are called **glaciers**. The ice in some glaciers is thousands of feet thick.

Ice History

Today, glaciers cover about one-tenth of Earth. Long ago, Earth was much cooler. More of it was covered with glaciers. These times were called ice ages.

The last great ice age ended about 10,000 years ago. Glaciers covered most of North America then.

4

Ice That Covers Earth

About one-tenth of Earth's land is permanently covered with ice. Can you guess which place has the most permanent ice today?

Place	Area in square miles (kilometers)
Antarctica	5,250,000 (12,588,000 square kilometers)
North Polar Regions (Greenland, Northern Canada, Arctic Ocean Islands)	799,000 (2,070,000 square kilometers)
Asia	44,000 (115,000 square kilometers)
Alaska and Rocky Mountains	29,700 (76,900 square kilometers)
South America	10,200 (26,500 square kilometers)
Iceland	4,699 (12,170 square kilometers)

It's a Fact

Scientists can learn a lot about Earth's history from glaciers. Over time, the ice in a glacier builds up layer upon layer. Scientists have drilled down more than two miles through a glacier in Antarctica.

The ice at the bottom of this hole formed about 420,000 years ago. Scientists are studying the little bubbles of air trapped in the ice. These bubbles can tell them what Earth's weather and air were like back then.

CHAPTER 1

How Glaciers Move

Glaciers move very slowly. Some move just two feet (.6 meter) per year. Still, they change the land that they cross. Some glaciers start to move high in the mountains. They scrape the mountaintops. They make them smooth. Other glaciers push through narrow **canyons** (KAN-yunz). These glaciers turn the canyons into wide valleys.

▲ Ruth Glacier is on the slopes of Mount McKinley, in Denali National Park, Alaska.

GLACIERS

The Ice Meets the Sea

Many glaciers end up in the sea. Big pieces of ice break off and fall into the water. Each big piece becomes an iceberg.

Today, the world's largest iceberg is about as big as the state of Rhode Island!

▲ Ice falls from a glacier into the sea.

▼ Some glaciers carve narrow, steep-sided inlets when they reach the ocean. These inlets are called fjords (fee-ORDZ). This fjord is in Norway.

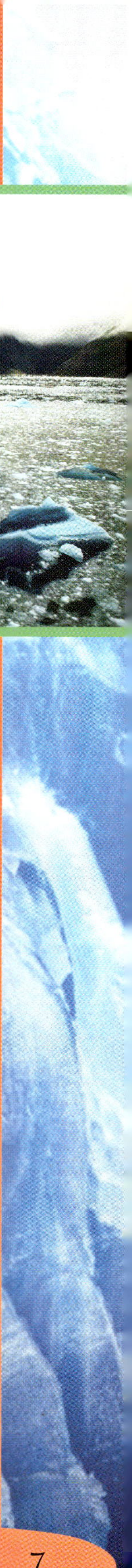

7

CHAPTER 1

After the Ice Melts

In winter, snow and ice sometimes make potholes in roads. Glaciers can do that, too. The holes are much bigger. How do glaciers do it?

Glaciers melt. The melted water gets trapped under the heavy ice. The ice pushes down on the water. Sometimes the water begins to spin. This spinning water can reach speeds of 125 miles (201 kilometers) per hour. The spinning water digs deep holes in the ground. These holes are called glacial potholes.

A melting glacier does something else. It leaves behind all the rocks and dirt it was carrying. The rocks and dirt form rows of low hills. The hills are shaped like eggs. They are called **drumlins**.

Sometimes a glacier carries a huge rock hundreds of miles. Then as it melts, it leaves the rock behind.

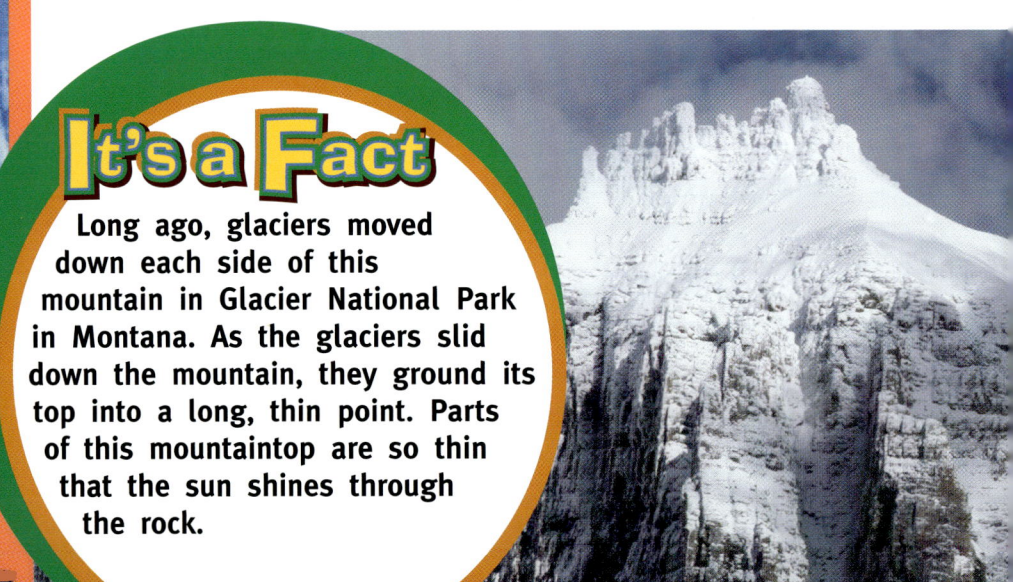

It's a Fact

Long ago, glaciers moved down each side of this mountain in Glacier National Park in Montana. As the glaciers slid down the mountain, they ground its top into a long, thin point. Parts of this mountaintop are so thin that the sun shines through the rock.

8

GLACIERS

▲ Long ago, a glacier dropped this huge boulder here.

◀ Spinning water dug this hole.

Everyday Science

Glaciers grind rock into dust. This dust is filled with minerals that help plants grow. Dust made by glaciers covers large parts of the midwestern United States. This dust makes the farmland very rich.

9

CHAPTER 2

Water

Glaciers are not the only cause of erosion. The water in rivers also causes it. Every river wears away the rock beneath it. Over time, rivers can cut canyons into solid rock.

Some types of rock are softer than others. A river will wear away soft rock faster than hard rock. The soft rock wears away in some rivers. What's left is a steep ledge of hard rock. River water falls over it. It's a waterfall!

Over time, the rushing water wears away the hard rock. The waterfall then moves slowly backward.

▲ The Colorado River helped carve out this canyon.

▲ Skogarfoss waterfall in Iceland

Solve This

Horseshoe Falls is about 40,000 feet up the Niagara River from Lake Erie. The falls move backward at 5 feet per year. How long will it take for the waterfall to move all the way to Lake Erie?

CHAPTER 2

The Grand Canyon

The Grand Canyon was formed by water. The Colorado River created it. It took five million years. The river had to wear down through rock one mile (1.6 kilometers) thick.

WATER

THEY MADE A DIFFERENCE

John Wesley Powell made the Grand Canyon famous. In 1869, Powell convinced nine men to join him on a trip down the Colorado River through the Grand Canyon. No one had ever made the trip before. No one had even tried.

Powell was a **geologist** (jee-AH-luh-jist). He learned much about the Grand Canyon during the trip. By the time the trip was over, he knew that the canyon had been eroded by the Colorado River.

◀ The amazing Grand Canyon stretches for 277 miles (446 kilometers) through northern Arizona. No wonder it took so long to create.

Solve This

The Grand Canyon is the most famous canyon in the world, but it is not the deepest. The Grand Canyon is about 5,000 feet (1,524 meters) deep. Cotahuasi Canyon in Peru is 11,000 feet (3,353 meters) deep. About how many times deeper is Cotahuasi than the Grand Canyon? Hint: Use estimation to find your answer.

CHAPTER 2

Snaking Rivers

Rivers change when they reach the bottom of a mountain. They are no longer going downhill. So they slow down. They get wider, too. The rivers wear away rock along their edges.

These slow, wide rivers can wind back and forth over flat ground. From the sky, these rivers look like snakes.

Where Rivers Dump Dirt

Rivers rush down mountains. As they go, they pick up lots of dirt and sand. Where does the dirt and sand go? Most of it is left at the spot where the river flows into the sea. This new land made from the dirt and sand is called a **delta**.

WATER

▲ The Mara River in Africa winds back and forth.

The Badlands

There are no rivers in Badlands National Park in South Dakota. But water still plays an important role in erosion there. This time, the water is rain. Rain collects in ditches called gullies. The rainwater races down the gullies, cutting into the soft rock and exposing the colorful rock below.

▼ round, striped hills in Badlands National Park

15

CHAPTER 2

▲ Many Egyptians still farm in the Nile Delta.

The Nile River runs through a desert. It carries lots of dirt along with it. Then it reaches the sea. All that dirt forms the Nile Delta. Its soil is very rich. People have farmed there for a long time.

Hazard Cave, ▶ Pickett State Park, Tennessee

Reread

Look again at the shapes that ice and water can make in the earth. What are some of the shapes made by glaciers? What are some of the shapes made by rivers?

16

WATER

Everyday Science

As rainwater seeps into the earth, it gets into cracks in underground rock. The moving water eats away at the soft rock. Over time, these cracks grow wider until they become caves.

The dripping water in caves leaves behind minerals. These minerals build up into amazing shapes. Some look like curtains. Others look like lace. Many are very beautiful.

17

CHAPTER 3

Wind

▲ Monument Valley in Arizona

Water is not the only thing that can change the shape of rock. Wind can change the shape of rock, too. How does wind do this?

Think of being at the beach on a windy day. The wind whips sand in your face. Those tiny bits of sand can erode solid rock.

The sand in wind can carve rocks into interesting shapes. A whole cliff can disappear. All that is left is a tall tower.

Careers in Science

People who study Earth are called geologists. Some geologists study how Earth formed. Others predict how it will look in the future. Some geologists look for ways to stop erosion in places where it might hurt people. They work to stop farmland from washing away or houses from sliding down cliffs.

CHAPTER 3

Shifting Dunes

In some deserts, the wind grinds all the loose rock down into sand. The sand gathers in huge piles. The piles are called **dunes** (DOONZ).

The wind blows the sand around. The dunes move and change shape. How do the dunes build up?

▼ The world's tallest sand dunes are in the Namib Desert in Africa. They rise as high as 1,300 feet (396 meters).

WIND

A dune needs an anchor. An anchor is something that is rooted in one place in the sand. It might be a rock or a tree. It could even be a tiny bit of grass.

Some sand piles up next to the anchor. It forms a mound. This mound becomes an anchor for even more sand. The dune grows larger.

▲ Sand is always on the move.

CHAPTER 3

Blown Away

We know that wind can wear away rock. So why doesn't the wind also blow away all the dirt? The answer is plants. The roots of plants hold the soil in place. What happens if the plants die?

In the 1930s, little rain fell across the central United States. Plants dried up and died. Few plants were left to hold the dirt in place. Wind blew the dirt into the air. It blew away three feet (.9 meter) of soil from farms. This time is known as the Dust Bowl.

▲ The wind created dust storms that were like blizzards. People had to keep their doors and windows shut tight to keep out the dust.

22

Digging Up Dinos

The wind sometimes uncovers amazing things as it wears away rock. **Fossils** are animal bones that have turned into rock. The Gobi Desert in Asia is one of the best places to find dinosaur fossils. Every year, fierce desert winds blast away at the rocks, exposing more fossils. A year later, the wind will have worn away those fossils, too.

CHAPTER 4

Wind and Water Work Together

▲ These stacks of rocks are in Victoria, Australia.

Wind and water sometimes work together. Waves pound against cliffs. The waves crack the rock. More waves carry away the loose rock.

At the same time, the wind blows against the cliffs. It wears them down, too.

Sometimes waves cut all the way through the cliffs. An arch forms. Together, the waves and wind wear the rock away. The top of the arch falls into the water. Only a tower of rock is left.

24

It's a Fact

Waves sometimes eat all the way through the top of a cave in a cliff, making a hole. This is called a blowhole. When waves smash into the cave, the water spouts up through the blowhole like a fountain.

CHAPTER 4

Sandy Beaches

Did you know that all sand used to be part of bigger rocks? Rocks fall off cliffs. They land in the ocean. Waves smash them. The pieces get smaller and smaller. They get so tiny that we call them sand.

Waves wash across the beach. They leave sand behind. Other waves carry the sand back out to sea. At the same time, the wind blows the sand around. Beaches are always changing because of the wind and waves.

▼ **Wind and waves constantly move the sand around.**

WIND AND WATER WORK TOGETHER

It's a Fact

Beaches come in lots of colors. They can be yellow, brown, pink, black, or white. It all depends on what the sand is made of. Pink beaches are made of tiny bits of seashells. Black beaches are made from crushed **volcanic** (vahl-KA-nik) rock and ash.

▲ This beach is on the island of Maui in Hawaii.

CHAPTER 4

Disappearing Beaches

Most people love the beach. Some love it so much that they want to live next to it. They build houses right at its edge.

Sometimes the beach in front of a group of houses starts to wear away. The water and wind keep moving the sand around. Some beaches lose three feet (.9 meter) of sand every year. What can people do about it?

▲ The Pacific Ocean eroded the beach under these houses.

WIND AND WATER WORK TOGETHER

Some people try to stop the beach from eroding. They put up seawalls. The walls stop waves from hitting the beach. They keep the sand from washing out to sea.

Other people dump new sand on the beach every year. They try to replace the sand that has washed away.

✓ POINT
Make Connections

What are some ways that erosion helps people? What are some ways that erosion makes life more difficult for people?

▲ seawall in Havana, Cuba

Conclusion

Earth is changing all the time. Erosion plays a big part in these changes. Wind, water, and ice smash rock. They carry it someplace new. They change the land.

Visit a beach. Watch the sand move as waves crash on the shore. Then remember that nothing can stop the power of erosion. Earth is always changing around you. Sometimes the changes are slow and take many years.

Type of Erosion	Result
Glaciers	U-shaped valleys fjords potholes
Water	canyons caves deltas
Wind	sand dunes towering desert rocks
Wind and Water	sea caves rock arches beaches

Glossary

canyon — (KAN-yun) a deep valley with high, steep sides (page 6)

delta — (DEL-tuh) an area of land at the mouth of a river (page 14)

drumlin — (DRUM-lun) an egg-shaped hill (page 8)

dune — (DOON) a mound or ridge of sand that has been piled up by the wind (page 20)

erosion — (ih-ROH-zhun) wearing away by wind, water, or ice (page 2)

fossil — (FAH-sul) a bone or print of an ancient plant or animal (page 23)

geologist — (jee-AH-luh-jist) a scientist who studies rocks or how Earth formed (page 13)

glacier — (GLAY-sher) a large, slowly moving chuck of ice (page 4)

volcanic — (vahl-KA-nik) made by a volcano (page 27)

Solve This

Answers

1. Page 11   8,000 years
2. Page 13   About 2 times deeper

Index

Appalachian Mountains, 2–3
Badlands National Park, 15
beach, 18, 26–30
blowhole, 25
canyon, 6, 10, 13, 30
cave, 16–17, 25, 30
Colorado River, 12–13
Cotahuasi Canyon, 13
delta, 14, 16, 30
dinosaur, 23
drumlin, 8
erosion, 2–3, 10, 15, 19, 29–30
fjord, 7, 30
fossil, 23
geologist, 13, 19
glacial pothole, 8
glacier, 4–10, 16, 30
Gobi Desert, 23
Grand Canyon, 12–13
ice age, 4
iceberg, 7
Namib Desert, 20
Nile River, 16
Powell, John Wesley, 13
river, 10–16
sand, 14, 18, 20–21, 26–30
sand dune, 20–21, 30
volcanic, 27
water, 2, 7–10, 12, 15, 17, 24–25, 28, 30
waterfall, 10–11
wave, 24–26, 29–30
wind, 2, 18, 20, 22–24, 26–28, 30